PLANT BASED

WHOLESOME RECIPES PACKED WITH VEGETABLES, GRAINS AND LEGUMES

pil

Publications International, Ltd.

Louis Weber, CEO
Publications International, Ltd.
8140 Lehigh Ave
Morton Grove, IL 60053

Photographs on front cover and pages 29 and 71 © Shutterstock.com.

Pictured on the front cover: Kale, Apple and Carrot Salad *(page 28)*.

Pictured on the back cover *(clockwise from top left):* Spinach Veggie Wrap *(page 92)*, Rainbow Vegetable Stew *(page 38)*, Garlic-Cilantro Green Beans *(page 118)* and Italian Bread Salad *(page 17)*.

ISBN: 978-1-64558-424-7

Manufactured in China.

8 7 6 5 4 3 2 1

Let's get social!

 @Publications_International

@PublicationsInternational

www.pilbooks.com

CONTENTS

Chapters:

Icon key:

NF nut free

Q quick prep

GF gluten free

EF egg free

V vegan

DF dairy free

MA make ahead

BREAKFAST & BRUNCH

Berry Buckwheat Scones

Makes 8 scones

1. Preheat oven to 375°F. Line baking sheet with parchment paper.

2. Combine all-purpose flour, ³/₄ cup buckwheat flour, palm sugar, baking powder and salt in bowl of food processor; pulse until combined. Add butter; pulse until pea-sized pieces of butter remain. Transfer mixture to large bowl; stir in berries.

3. Whisk egg and cream in small bowl. Stir cream mixture into flour mixture until soft dough forms.

4. Transfer dough to work surface lightly dusted with buckwheat flour; gently pat into an 8-inch round about ³/₄ inch thick. Cut into 8 wedges.

5. Place wedges 1¹/₂ inches apart on prepared baking sheet. Sprinkle tops with turbinado sugar, if desired. Bake 20 to 25 minutes or until golden. Remove to wire rack; cool 10 minutes.

6. Serve warm with jam or lemon curd, if desired.

- 1¹/₄ **cups all-purpose flour**
- ³/₄ **cup buckwheat flour, plus additional for dusting**
- ¹/₄ **cup palm sugar or packed brown sugar**
- 1 **tablespoon baking powder**
- ¹/₂ **teaspoon salt**
- ¹/₂ **cup (1 stick) cold butter, cubed**
- ³/₄ **cup fresh raspberries**
- ³/₄ **cup fresh blackberries**
- 1 **egg**
- ¹/₂ **cup whipping cream**
- 1 **tablespoon turbinado sugar (optional)**
- **Jam or lemon curd (optional)**

BREAKFAST & BRUNCH

Cranberry Buttermilk Pancakes

Makes 18 (3-inch) pancakes

1 cup all-purpose flour

1 cup whole wheat flour

2 teaspoons baking powder

1 teaspoon baking soda

1/2 teaspoon salt

1/2 teaspoon ground cinnamon

1/4 teaspoon ground nutmeg

2/3 cup whole berry cranberry sauce

2 eggs

2 tablespoons vegetable oil, plus additional for cooking

1 1/2 cups buttermilk

Maple syrup (optional)

1. Combine all-purpose flour, whole wheat flour, baking powder, baking soda, cinnamon and nutmeg in small bowl; mix well. Whisk cranberry sauce, eggs and 2 tablespoons oil in large bowl until well blended. Gradually stir in flour mixture until combined. Stir in buttermilk until smooth and well blended.

2. Heat large nonstick griddle or skillet over medium heat. Brush with oil. Pour 1/4 cupfuls of batter 2 inches apart onto griddle. Cook 3 minutes or until lightly browned and edges begin to bubble. Turn over; cook 3 minutes or until lightly browned. Repeat with remaining batter. Serve with maple syrup, if desired.

BREAKFAST & BRUNCH

Banana-Blueberry Oat and Quinoa Cake

Makes 12 to 16 servings

2 cups old-fashioned oats

1 cup uncooked quinoa, rinsed well in fine-mesh strainer

1 cup packed dark brown sugar or palm sugar, divided

$^2/_3$ cup all-purpose flour

$1^1/_2$ teaspoons ground cinnamon

$1^1/_2$ teaspoons baking powder

$^1/_2$ teaspoon salt

3 medium ripe bananas

1 cup milk

2 eggs

$^1/_2$ cup applesauce

2 tablespoons butter, melted

$^1/_2$ teaspoon vanilla

2 cups fresh blueberries, divided

$^1/_2$ cup chopped pecans

1. Preheat oven to 375°F. Spray 13×9-inch baking pan with nonstick cooking spray.

2. Combine oats, quinoa, $^3/_4$ cup brown sugar, flour, cinnamon, baking powder and salt in large bowl.

3. Mash bananas in medium bowl. Stir in milk, eggs, applesauce, butter and vanilla. Add to quinoa mixture; mix well. Fold in 1 cup blueberries. Spread batter in prepared pan; sprinkle with remaining blueberries, remaining $^1/_4$ cup brown sugar and pecans.

4. Bake 40 to 45 minutes or until golden brown and set. Cool in pan 10 minutes. Serve warm or at room temperature. Store leftovers in refrigerator.

BREAKFAST & BRUNCH

Baked Pumpkin Oatmeal

Makes 6 servings

2 cups old-fashioned oats

2 cups milk

1 cup canned pumpkin

2 eggs

¹/₃ cup packed brown sugar or palm sugar

1 teaspoon vanilla

¹/₂ cup dried cranberries, plus additional for topping

1 teaspoon pumpkin pie spice

¹/₂ teaspoon salt

¹/₂ teaspoon baking powder

Maple syrup

Chopped pecans (optional)

1. Preheat oven to 350°F. Spray 8-inch square baking dish with nonstick cooking spray.

2. Spread oats on ungreased baking sheet. Bake about 10 minutes or until fragrant and lightly browned, stirring occasionally. Pour into medium bowl; let cool slightly.

3. Whisk milk, pumpkin, eggs, brown sugar and vanilla in large bowl until well blended. Add ¹/₂ cup cranberries, pumpkin pie spice, salt and baking powder to oats; mix well. Add oat mixture to pumpkin mixture; stir until well blended. Pour into prepared baking dish.

4. Bake about 45 minutes or until top is set and knife inserted into center comes out almost clean. Serve warm with maple syrup, additional cranberries and pecans, if desired. Store leftovers in the refrigerator. Reheat individual servings in the microwave.

Gluten-Free: To make sure this recipe is gluten-free, select gluten-free oats that have been processed in a dedicated gluten-free facility.

BREAKFAST & BRUNCH

Raisin-Nut Oatmeal

Makes 4 servings

3³/₄ cups water

2²/₃ cups old-fashioned oats

²/₃ cup raisins

¹/₂ cup sliced almonds, toasted*

¹/₃ cup palm sugar or packed brown sugar

¹/₂ teaspoon salt

¹/₂ teaspoon ground cinnamon

¹/₈ teaspoon ground ginger

*To toast almonds, spread in single layer in small heavy skill. Cook over medium heat 2 to 3 minutes or until nuts are lightly browned, stirring frequently. Cool before using.

1. Bring water to a boil in large saucepan over high heat. Stir in remaining ingredients.

2. Reduce heat to medium. Cook and stir 4 to 5 minutes or until thick and creamy.

Note: For richer oatmeal, substitute 2 cups dairy-free or regular milk for 2 cups of the water.

Q GF EF V DF

Oatmeal Waffles with Spiced Apple Compote

Makes 6 servings

APPLE COMPOTE

- 2 **tablespoons butter**
- 1 **pound Granny Smith apples, peeled and cut into ¹/₂-inch pieces**
- ¹/₄ **cup maple syrup**
- ¹/₂ **cup water**
- ¹/₄ **cup raisins**
- 1 **teaspoon ground cinnamon**

WAFFLES

- 1¹/₄ **cups quick-cooking oats**
- ³/₄ **cup oat flour**
- ¹/₄ **cup ground flaxseed**
- 1 **tablespoon baking powder**
- ¹/₂ **teaspoon salt**
- 1³/₄ **cups milk, heated**
- ¹/₂ **cup (1 stick) butter, melted and cooled slightly**
- 3 **eggs**
- ¹/₄ **cup maple syrup**

1. Preheat oven to 200°F. Set wire rack on top of large baking sheet; place in oven.

2. For compote, melt 2 tablespoons butter in large nonstick skillet over medium-high heat. Add apples, ¹/₄ cup maple syrup, water, raisins and cinnamon; mix well. Reduce heat to medium. Cover and cook 5 minutes. Uncover; continue cooking 5 minutes or until apples are tender and most of liquid has evaporated, stirring occasionally. Set aside.

3. For waffles, combine oats, flour, flaxseed, baking powder and salt in large bowl. Pour in hot milk; stir until combined. Let stand 5 minutes.

4. Whisk melted butter, eggs and ¹/₄ cup maple syrup in medium bowl. Pour into oat mixture; stir until combined.

5. Preheat Belgian waffle maker to medium-high heat. Pour ¹/₃ cup batter into each well of waffle maker. Close lid; cook 6 minutes or until golden brown. Remove waffles to wire rack in oven; tent with foil to keep warm. Repeat with remaining batter.

6. Serve waffles with apple compote.

FRESH SALADS

Italian Bread Salad

Makes 4 servings

1. Preheat oven to 400°F. Spread bread cubes on baking sheet. Bake 5 to 7 minutes or until lightly toasted and dry, stirring occasionally. Remove to bowl; let cool.

2. Whisk buttermilk, garlic, dill, onion powder, ¼ teaspoon salt and pepper in small bowl until well blended. Let stand 15 minutes to allow flavors to blend.

3. Spoon equal amounts of bread cubes into bottom of four (1-pint) resealable jars. Layer tomatoes, cucumber, celery and basil over bread. Sprinkle with additional salt, if desired.

4. Stir dressing; pour equal amounts over salads. Seal jars; shake to distribute dressing. Refrigerate until ready to serve.

- 4 slices Italian bread, cut into ½-inch cubes (about 4 cups)
- ½ cup buttermilk
- 1 clove garlic, minced
- 1 tablespoon minced fresh dill **or** 1 teaspoon dried dill weed
- 1½ teaspoons onion powder
- ¼ teaspoon salt, plus additional as needed
- ¼ teaspoon black pepper
- ½ cup cherry or grape tomatoes, quartered
- 1 cucumber, peeled, cut in half lengthwise, seeded and thinly sliced
- 1 stalk celery, thinly sliced
- 2 tablespoons minced fresh basil

FRESH SALADS

Warm Brussels Sprouts Salad with Mustard Vinaigrette

Makes 4 servings

- 3 **cups brussels sprouts, cut into quarters**
- 1 **pint (2 cups) grape tomatoes**
- ½ **cup sliced red onion**
- 3 **tablespoons olive oil, divided**
- 2 **tablespoons balsamic vinegar, divided**
- ¼ **teaspoon salt**
- 1 **tablespoon water**
- 2 **teaspoons Dijon mustard**
- 1 **teaspoon honey**
- 4 **cups chopped butter lettuce**
- ¼ **cup shaved Parmesan cheese**

1. Preheat oven to 375°F.

2. Combine brussels sprouts, tomatoes and onion in large bowl. Add 1 tablespoon oil, 1 tablespoon vinegar and salt; toss to coat evenly. Arrange in single layer on baking sheet.

3. Bake 20 minutes or until brussels sprouts are browned and tender, stirring once. Let stand 10 minutes to cool slightly.

4. Meanwhile, whisk remaining 2 tablespoons oil, 1 tablespoon vinegar, water, mustard and honey in large bowl until smooth and well blended. Add vegetables; toss to coat evenly.

5. Arrange lettuce on 4 plates. Spoon vegetables evenly over lettuce. Top with cheese.

Vegan: Omit Parmesan cheese and substitute agave nectar or maple syrup for the honey.

FRESH SALADS

Superfood Kale Salad

Makes 4 servings

CARROTS

- 8 **carrots, trimmed**
- 2 **tablespoons maple syrup**
- 2 **tablespoons olive oil**
- 1/2 **teaspoon salt**
- 1/8 **teaspoon black pepper**
- **Dash ground red pepper**

VINAIGRETTE

- 1/4 **cup olive oil**
- 2 **tablespoons maple syrup**
- 3 **tablespoons lemon juice**
- 3/4 **teaspoon grated lemon peel**
- 1/2 **teaspoon salt**
- 1/8 **teaspoon black pepper**

SALAD

- 4 **cups chopped kale**
- 2 **cups chopped mixed greens**
- 1 **cup dried cranberries**
- 1 **cup slivered almonds, toasted***
- 1 **cup shredded Parmesan cheese**

*To toast almonds, spread on ungreased baking sheet. Bake in preheated 350°F oven 6 to 8 minutes or until lightly browned, stirring occasionally.

1. Preheat oven to 400°F. Line baking sheet with parchment paper.

2. Place carrots on prepared baking sheet. Whisk 2 tablespoons maple syrup, 2 tablespoons oil, 1/2 teaspoon salt, 1/8 teaspoon black pepper and red pepper in small bowl until well blended. Brush some of oil mixture over carrots. Roast 30 minutes or until carrots are tender, brushing with oil mixture and shaking pan every 10 minutes. Slice crosswise into coins when carrots are cool enough to handle.

3. While carrots are roasting, prepare vinaigrette. Whisk 1/4 cup oil, 2 tablespoons maple syrup, lemon juice, lemon peel, 1/2 teaspoon salt and 1/8 teaspoon black pepper in small bowl until well blended.

4. Combine kale, greens, cranberries, almonds and cheese in large bowl. Add carrots. Pour vinaigrette over salad; toss to coat.

Vegan: Omit Parmesan cheese.

Make Ahead: Substitute additional kale for the spring greens or plan on adding the spring greens just before serving. Kale stands up well to being dressed ahead of time, whereas spring greens get soft very quickly.

FRESH SALADS

Asparagus and Arugula Salad

Makes 4 to 6 servings

- 1/2 cup sun-dried tomatoes (not packed in oil)
- 1 cup boiling water
- 1 cup sliced asparagus (1-inch pieces)
- 1 package (5 ounces) baby arugula (4 cups)
- 1/2 cup shaved Parmesan cheese
- 1/4 cup extra virgin olive oil
- 2 tablespoons lemon juice
- 1 tablespoon orange juice
- 1 clove garlic, minced
- 1/2 teaspoon salt
- 1/2 teaspoon grated lemon peel
- 1/8 teaspoon black pepper (optional)

1. Place sun-dried tomatoes in small bowl; pour boiling water over tomatoes. Let stand 5 minutes; drain well.

2. Bring medium saucepan of salted water to a boil. Add asparagus; cook 1 minute or until crisp-tender. Rinse under cold water to stop cooking.

3. Combine arugula, asparagus, sun-dried tomatoes and cheese in large bowl. Whisk oil, lemon juice, orange juice, garlic, salt, lemon peel and pepper, if desired, in small bowl until well blended. Pour over salad; toss gently to coat.

Vegan: Omit Parmesan cheese.

FRESH SALADS

Cabbage and Red Potato Salad with Cilantro-Lime Dressing

Makes 4 servings

- **12 ounces baby red potatoes, quartered and cooked**
- **³/4 teaspoon salt, divided**
- **¹/2 cup finely chopped fresh cilantro**
- **2 tablespoons lime juice**
- **2 tablespoons extra virgin olive oil**
- **2 teaspoons maple syrup**
- **¹/2 teaspoon ground cumin**
- **2 cups sliced napa cabbage**
- **2 cups sliced red cabbage**
- **¹/2 cup sliced green onions**
- **2 tablespoons sunflower kernels**

1. Place potatoes in medium saucepan. Add water to cover and ¹/2 teaspoon salt. Bring to a boil. Reduce heat; simmer 10 to 15 minutes or until potatoes are tender. Drain and rinse under cold water to stop cooking.

2. Whisk cilantro, lime juice, oil, maple syrup, cumin and remaining ¹/4 teaspoon salt in small bowl until smooth and well blended. Let stand 30 minutes to allow flavors to blend.

3. Combine napa cabbage, red cabbage, potatoes and green onions in large bowl; mix well. Add dressing; toss to coat evenly. Sprinkle with sunflower kernels just before serving.

FRESH SALADS

Spinach Salad

Makes 4 servings

DRESSING

- ¼ **cup balsamic vinegar**
- 1 **clove garlic, minced**
- ½ **teaspoon sugar**
- ¼ **teaspoon salt**
- ⅛ **teaspoon black pepper**
- ¼ **cup extra virgin olive oil**
- ¼ **cup vegetable oil**

SALAD

- 8 **cups packed baby spinach**
- 1 **cup diced tomatoes**
- 1 **cup drained mandarin oranges**
- 1 **cup glazed pecans***
- ½ **cup crumbled feta cheese**
- ½ **cup diced red onion**
- ½ **cup dried cranberries**
- 1 **can (3 ounces) crispy rice noodles****
- 4 **teaspoons toasted sesame seeds**

Glazed pecans can be found in the produce section of many supermarkets (with other salad toppings). Or make them yourself. (See Tip.)

**Crispy rice noodles can be found with canned chow mein noodles in the Asian section of the supermarket.*

1. For dressing, whisk vinegar, garlic, sugar, salt and pepper in medium bowl until blended. Whisk in olive oil and vegetable oil in thin steady stream until well blended.

2. Divide spinach among 4 serving bowls. Top evenly with tomatoes, oranges, pecans, cheese, onion and cranberries. Sprinkle with rice noodles and sesame seeds. Drizzle each salad with 3 tablespoons dressing.

Tip: To make glazed pecans, combine 1 cup pecan halves, ¼ cup sugar, 1 tablespoon butter and ½ teaspoon salt in medium skillet; cook and stir over medium heat 5 minutes or until sugar mixture is dark brown and nuts are well coated. Spread on large plate; cool completely. Break into pieces or coarsely chop.

Vegan: Omit feta cheese.

FRESH SALADS

Kale, Apple and Carrot Salad

Makes 4 servings

DRESSING

- ¼ **cup red wine vinegar**
- 2 **tablespoons minced shallot**
- 1 **tablespoon honey**
- ¼ **teaspoon salt**
- ⅛ **teaspoon black pepper**
- ¼ **cup extra virgin olive oil**
- 2 **tablespoons vegetable oil**

SALAD

- 1 **tablespoon olive oil**
- 2 **carrots, cut into ¼-inch slices**
- 1 **tablespoon honey**
- **Salt and black pepper**
- 6 **cups chopped kale**
- ½ **cup pecan halves**
- ½ **cup dried cranberries**
- ¼ **cup roasted salted pumpkin seeds (pepitas)**
- ¼ **cup pine nuts**
- 8 **dried dates, halved or chopped**
- 2 **apples, halved and thinly sliced**

1. For dressing, whisk vinegar, shallot, 1 tablespoon honey, ¼ teaspoon salt and ⅛ teaspoon pepper in medium bowl until well blended. Whisk in ¼ cup olive oil and vegetable oil in thin steady stream until well blended.

2. For salad, heat 1 tablespoon olive oil in medium skillet over medium-high heat. Add carrots; cook and stir 8 to 10 minutes or until carrots are crisp-tender. Stir in 1 tablespoon honey; season with salt and pepper. Cool completely.

3. Place kale in large bowl. Top with pecans, cranberries, pumpkin seeds, pine nuts and dates; toss gently to blend. Top with carrots and apples. Serve with dressing.

FRESH SALADS

Taco Salad To Go

Makes 4 (1-quart) jars

DRESSING

- ¼ **cup mayonnaise**
- ¼ **cup plain yogurt or sour cream**
- 1 **tablespoon lime juice**
- ½ **teaspoon chipotle chili powder**
- 1 **clove garlic, minced**
- ¼ **cup crumbled cotija, feta or Parmesan cheese**
- ¼ **cup chopped fresh cilantro**

SALAD

- 1 **tablespoon vegetable oil**
- 1 **package (16 ounces) frozen corn**
- ¼ **teaspoon salt**
- 1 **large avocado, diced**
- 1 **teaspoon lime juice**
- 1 **can (15 ounces) black beans, rinsed and drained**
- 2 **medium tomatoes, seeded and diced**
- ½ **cup finely chopped red onion**
- **Packaged corn tortilla strips or chips**
- **Chopped fresh lettuce or spinach**

1. For dressing, whisk mayonnaise, yogurt, 1 tablespoon lime juice, chili powder and garlic in small bowl. Stir in cheese and cilantro.

2. For salad, heat oil in saucepan over high heat. Add corn; cook 10 to 15 minutes or until lightly browned, stirring occasionally. Stir in salt. Transfer to medium bowl; cool to room temperature. Combine avocado and 1 teaspoon lime juice in small bowl; toss to coat.

3. For each 1-quart jar, layer 2½ tablespoons dressing, ½ cup corn, scant ½ cup black beans, ¼ cup tomatoes, 2 tablespoons onion and about ¼ cup avocado. Top with tortilla strips and lettuce. Seal jars.

4. Refrigerate until ready to serve.

Note: You can also make these without the lettuce. If so, use four (1-pint) jars.

FRESH SALADS

Mediterranean Barley Salad

Makes 4 servings

1¹/₃ cups water

¹/₂ teaspoon salt

²/₃ cup uncooked quick-cooking pearl barley

1 can (14 ounces) quartered artichoke hearts, drained and coarsely chopped

2 medium tomatoes, seeded and chopped

¹/₄ cup chopped fresh parsley

1 tablespoon extra virgin olive oil

1 tablespoon Greek seasoning

1 teaspoon grated lemon peel

2 tablespoons lemon juice

1 package (4 ounces) feta cheese, crumbled

Salt and black pepper

1. Bring water and ¹/₂ teaspoon salt to a boil in medium saucepan. Stir in barley. Reduce heat; cover and simmer 10 to 12 minutes or until tender.

2. Meanwhile, combine artichokes, tomatoes, parsley, oil, Greek seasoning, lemon peel and lemon juice in large bowl. Toss gently to blend.

3. Drain barley; rinse under cold water to cool quickly; drain well.

4. Add barley to artichoke mixture; toss well. Add cheese; toss gently to blend Season with salt and pepper.

Vegan: Omit cheese.

   NF Q EF MA

SOUPS & STEWS

Cream of Asparagus Soup

Makes 6 to 8 servings

1. Trim off and discard tough ends of asparagus. Cut asparagus into 1-inch pieces. Combine asparagus and 1 cup broth in medium saucepan; cook 12 to 15 minutes or until tender.

2. Remove 1 cup asparagus pieces; reserve. Process remaining asparagus pieces with broth in blender or food processor until smooth.

3. Melt butter in large saucepan. Stir in flour until smooth. Gradually add remaining 2 1/2 cups broth; cook until slightly thickened, stirring occasionally. Stir in cream, salt, pepper, asparagus mixture and reserved asparagus pieces; cook until heated through.

1 **pound asparagus**

3 1/2 **cups vegetable broth, divided**

1/4 **cup (1/2 stick) butter**

1/4 **cup all-purpose flour**

1/2 **cup whipping cream or milk**

1/2 **teaspoon salt**

1/8 **teaspoon black pepper**

SOUPS & STEWS

Minestrone Soup

Makes 4 to 6 servings

1 tablespoon olive oil

¹/₂ cup chopped onion

1 stalk celery, diced

1 carrot, diced

2 cloves garlic, minced

4 cups vegetable broth

1 bay leaf

³/₄ teaspoon salt

¹/₂ teaspoon dried basil

¹/₂ teaspoon dried oregano

¹/₄ teaspoon dried thyme

¹/₄ teaspoon sugar

Black pepper

1 can (15 ounces) dark red kidney beans, rinsed and drained

1 can (15 ounces) navy beans or cannellini beans, rinsed and drained

1 can (about 14 ounces) diced tomatoes

1 cup diced zucchini

¹/₂ cup uncooked small shell pasta

¹/₂ cup frozen cut green beans

¹/₄ cup dry red wine

1 cup packed chopped fresh spinach

1. Heat oil in large saucepan or Dutch oven over medium-high heat. Add onion, celery, carrot and garlic; cook and stir 5 to 7 minutes or until vegetables are tender. Add broth, bay leaf, salt, basil, oregano, thyme, sugar and pepper; bring to a boil.

2. Stir in kidney beans, navy beans, tomatoes, zucchini, pasta, green beans and wine; cook 10 minutes, stirring occasionally.

3. Add spinach; cook 2 minutes or until pasta and zucchini are tender.

Gluten-Free: Use any small shape of gluten-free pasta instead of regular shell pasta.

SOUPS & STEWS

Rainbow Vegetable Stew

Makes 4 to 6 servings

1 tablespoon olive oil

1 red onion, chopped

2 stalks celery, chopped

3 cloves garlic, minced

2 teaspoons salt, divided

4 cups vegetable broth

1 butternut squash (about 2 pounds) peeled and cut into ½-inch cubes

1 red bell pepper, chopped

1 green bell pepper, chopped

1 teaspoon ground cumin

½ teaspoon dried oregano

¼ teaspoon chipotle chili powder

¾ cup uncooked tricolor or white quinoa

1½ cups water

½ cup corn

1 can (15 ounces) black beans, rinsed and drained

½ cup chopped fresh parsley

1 tablespoon lime juice

1. Heat oil in large saucepan over medium-high heat. Add onion and celery; cook and stir 5 minutes or until vegetables are softened. Add garlic and 1½ teaspoons salt; cook and stir 30 seconds. Stir in broth, squash, bell peppers, cumin, oregano and chili powder; bring to a boil. Reduce heat to medium; simmer 20 minutes or until squash is tender.

2. Rinse quinoa in fine mesh strainer under cold water. Meanwhile, bring 1½ cups water, quinoa and remaining ½ teaspoon salt to a boil in medium saucepan. Reduce heat to low; cover and simmer 15 minutes or until quinoa is tender and water is absorbed.

3. Stir corn and beans into stew; cook 5 minutes or until heated through. Stir in parsley and lime juice. Serve with quinoa.

SOUPS & STEWS

Garden Vegetable Soup

Makes 8 to 10 servings

1 tablespoon olive oil

1 medium onion, chopped

1 carrot, chopped

1 stalk celery, chopped

1 medium zucchini, diced

1 medium yellow squash, diced

1 red bell pepper, diced

2 tablespoons tomato paste

2 cloves garlic, minced

2 teaspoons salt

1 teaspoon Italian seasoning

1/2 teaspoon black pepper

8 cups vegetable broth

1 can (28 ounces) whole tomatoes, chopped, juice reserved

1/2 cup uncooked pearl barley

1 cup cut green beans (1-inch pieces)

1/2 cup corn

1/4 cup slivered fresh basil

1 tablespoon lemon juice

1. Heat oil in large saucepan or Dutch oven over medium-high heat. Add onion, carrot and celery; cook and stir 8 minutes or until vegetables are softened. Add zucchini, yellow squash and bell pepper; cook and stir 5 minutes or until softened. Stir in tomato paste, garlic, salt, Italian seasoning and black pepper; cook 1 minute. Stir in broth and tomatoes with juice; bring to a boil. Stir in barley.

2. Reduce heat to low; cook 30 minutes. Stir in green beans and corn; cook about 15 minutes or until barley is tender and green beans are crisp-tender. Stir in basil and lemon juice.

NF EF V DF MA

SOUPS & STEWS

Lentil-Barley Soup

Makes 8 servings

1 tablespoon olive oil

½ cup chopped onion

½ cup chopped celery

1 teaspoon minced garlic

4 cups vegetable broth

2 cups water

1 can (28 ounces) diced tomatoes

¾ cup uncooked pearl barley

¾ cup dried lentils, rinsed and sorted

1 tablespoon fresh oregano *or* 1 teaspoon dried oregano

1½ teaspoons fresh rosemary *or* ½ teaspoon dried rosemary

1 teaspoon lemon-pepper seasoning

1 cup thinly sliced carrots

1 cup (4 ounces) shredded Swiss or mozzarella cheese

1. Heat oil in large saucepan over medium heat. Add onion and celery; cook and stir 5 minutes or until softened. Add garlic; cook and stir 30 seconds.

2. Add broth, water, tomatoes, barley, lentils, oregano, rosemary and lemon-pepper seasoning. Bring to a boil over high heat. Reduce heat; cover and simmer 45 minutes or until barley and lentils are tender, stirring occasionally.

3. Add carrots; cover and simmer 15 minutes or until carrots are tender and soup is thickened. Sprinkle with cheese just before serving.

Vegan: Omit cheese.

SOUPS & STEWS

Ribollita (Tuscan Bread Soup)

Makes 6 to 8 servings

- 2 tablespoons olive oil
- 1 onion, halved and thinly sliced
- 2 stalks celery, diced
- 1 large carrot, julienned
- 3 cloves garlic, minced
- 2 medium zucchini, halved lengthwise and thinly sliced
- 1 yellow squash, halved lengthwise and thinly sliced
- 1 can (28 ounces) whole tomatoes, undrained
- 1 can (15 ounces) cannellini beans, rinsed and drained
- 1½ teaspoons salt
- 1 teaspoon Italian seasoning
- ¼ teaspoon black pepper
- 1 bay leaf
- ¼ teaspoon red pepper flakes (optional)
- 4 cups vegetable broth
- 2 cups water
- 1 bunch kale, stemmed and coarsely chopped or 3 cups thinly sliced cabbage
- 8 ounces Tuscan or rustic bread, cubed

1. Heat oil in large saucepan over medium-high heat. Add onion, celery and carrot; cook and stir 5 minutes. Add garlic, zucchini and yellow squash; cook and stir 5 minutes.

2. Add tomatoes with juice, beans, salt, Italian seasoning, black pepper, bay leaf and red pepper flakes, if desired. Add broth and water; bring to a boil. Reduce heat; simmer 15 minutes. Add kale and bread; simmer 10 minutes or until vegetables are tender, bread is soft and soup is thick.

Note: This is a great recipe to use a spiralizer if you have one. Use the spiral slicing blade to spiral the zucchini and yellow squash, then cut in half to make half moon slices. Use the thin ribbon blade to spiral the onion and carrot, and then cut into desired lengths.

SOUPS & STEWS

Italian Escarole and White Bean Stew

Makes 4 servings

1 head escarole (about 12 ounces)

1 tablespoon olive oil

1 onion, chopped

3 carrots, cut into ½-inch-thick rounds

2 cloves garlic, minced

1 can (about 14 ounces) vegetable broth

2 cans (about 15 ounces each) Great Northern white beans, rinsed and drained

¼ teaspoon red pepper flakes

Salt

Grated Parmesan cheese (optional)

1. Trim base of escarole. Roughly cut crosswise into 1-inch-wide strips. Wash well in large bowl of cold water. Lift out by handfuls, leaving sand or dirt in bottom of bowl. Shake to remove excess water, but do not dry. Place in medium bowl.

2. Heat oil in large saucepan over medium-high heat. Add onion and carrots; cook and stir about 5 minutes or until onion is softened. Add garlic; cook and stir 1 minute. Add broth; bring to a boil. Stir in beans, escarole and red pepper flakes.

3. Reduce heat to low; cover and simmer 30 minutes or until escarole is wilted and very tender. Season with salt. Sprinkle with Parmesan, if desired.

Vegan: Omit Parmesan cheese.

SOUPS & STEWS

Barley Stew with Cornmeal-Cheese Dumplings

Makes 4 servings

STEW

- 2 cans (11$\frac{1}{2}$ ounces each) spicy vegetable juice cocktail
- 1 can (15 ounces) butter beans, drained
- 1 can (about 14 ounces) diced tomatoes
- 1 cup sliced zucchini
- 1 cup sliced carrots
- 1 cup water
- $\frac{1}{2}$ cup chopped peeled parsnip
- $\frac{1}{3}$ cup quick pearl barley
- 1 bay leaf
- 2 tablespoons chopped fresh thyme
- 1$\frac{1}{2}$ tablespoons chopped fresh rosemary leaves
- $\frac{1}{2}$ teaspoon salt

DUMPLINGS

- $\frac{1}{3}$ cup all-purpose flour
- $\frac{1}{3}$ cup cornmeal
- 1 teaspoon baking powder
- $\frac{1}{4}$ cup milk
- 1 tablespoon canola oil
- $\frac{1}{3}$ cup shredded Cheddar cheese

1. Combine vegetable juice, beans, tomatoes with juice, zucchini, carrots, water, parsnip, barley, bay leaf, thyme and rosemary in large saucepan. Bring to a boil over high heat. Reduce heat to medium-low. Cover; simmer 20 to 25 minutes or until tender, stirring occasionally. Remove and discard bay leaf.

2. Combine flour, cornmeal and baking powder in small bowl. Combine milk and oil in separate small bowl; stir into flour mixture. Stir in cheese. Drop dough by spoonfuls to make 4 mounds onto boiling stew. Cover and simmer 10 to 12 minutes or until wooden toothpick inserted near center of dumplings comes out clean.

Tip: To make ahead, prepare stew ahead through step 1. Reheat in large saucepan; prepare dumplings when stew is hot and follow directions in step 2.

SOUPS & STEWS

Curried Ginger Pumpkin Soup

Makes 8 servings

1 tablespoon
vegetable oil

1 large onion, coarsely
chopped

1 large Golden
Delicious apple,
peeled and coarsely
chopped

3 slices (¼-inch)
peeled fresh ginger

1½ teaspoons curry
powder

2½ to 3 cups vegetable
broth, divided

2 cans (15 ounces each)
pumpkin purée

1 cup canned coconut
milk

1 teaspoon salt

Black pepper

Roasted salted
pumpkin seeds
(pepitas)

1. Heat oil in large saucepan over medium heat. Add onion, apple, ginger and curry powder; cook and stir 10 minutes. Add ½ cup broth; cover and simmer 10 minutes or until apple is tender.

2. Pour onion mixture into blender; blend until smooth. Return to saucepan. (Or use hand-held immersion blender.)

3. Add pumpkin, 2 cups broth, coconut milk, salt and pepper; cook until heated through, stirring occasionally. If soup is too thick, add additional broth, a few tablespoons at a time, until soup reaches desired consistency. Sprinkle with pumpkin seeds, if desired.

SMALL PLATES

Crostini with Lemony Pesto

Makes 16 crostini

1. Preheat oven to 350°F.

2. Cut baguette crosswise into 16 slices; arrange on baking sheet. Bake 11 to 12 minutes or until bread begins to brown. Cool completely.

3. Combine pesto and lemon juice in small bowl; stir until well blended. Spread each bread slice with $\frac{1}{2}$ teaspoon pesto mixture. Top with tomato. Serve immediately.

1 (4-ounce) French baguette

3 tablespoons prepared pesto

$\frac{1}{2}$ teaspoon lemon juice

$\frac{1}{2}$ cup chopped plum tomato

SMALL PLATES

Cauliflower Tacos with Chipotle Crema

Makes 8 tacos

- 1 package (8 ounces) sliced cremini mushrooms
- 4 tablespoons olive oil, divided
- 1³/₄ teaspoons salt, divided
- 1 head cauliflower
- 1 teaspoon ground cumin
- ¹/₂ teaspoon dried oregano
- ¹/₄ teaspoon ground coriander
- ¹/₄ teaspoon ground cinnamon
- ¹/₄ teaspoon black pepper
- ¹/₂ cup vegan sour cream
- 2 teaspoons lime juice
- ¹/₂ teaspoon chipotle chili powder
- ¹/₂ cup vegetarian refried beans
- 8 taco-size corn tortillas
- Chopped fresh cilantro (optional)
- Pickled Red Onions (recipe follows) or sliced red onion

1. Preheat oven to 400°F. Toss mushrooms with 1 tablespoon oil and ¹/₄ teaspoon salt in large bowl. Spread on small baking sheet.

2. Remove leaves from cauliflower. Remove florets; cut into 1-inch pieces. Place in same large bowl. Add remaining 3 tablespoons oil, 1 teaspoon salt, cumin, oregano, coriander, cinnamon and black pepper; mix well. Spread on sheet pan in single layer.

3. Roast cauliflower about 40 minutes or until browned and tender, stirring a few times. Roast mushrooms 20 minutes or until dry and browned, stirring once.

4. For crema, combine sour cream, lime juice, chili powder and remaining ¹/₂ teaspoon salt in small bowl.

5. For each taco, spread 1 tablespoon beans over tortilla; spread 1 teaspoon crema over beans. Top with about 3 mushroom slices and ¹/₄ cup cauliflower. Top with cilantro and red onions, if desired. Fold in half.

Pickled Red Onions: Thinly slice 1 small red onion; place in large glass jar. Add ¹/₄ cup white wine vinegar or distilled white vinegar, 2 tablespoons water, 1 teaspoon sugar and 1 teaspoon salt. Seal jar; shake well. Refrigerate at least 1 hour or up to 1 week. Makes about ¹/₂ cup.

  EF

SMALL PLATES

Fried Zucchini

Makes 4 to 6 servings

2 medium zucchini (about 10 ounces each)

¼ cup all-purpose flour

½ teaspoon salt

½ teaspoon dried oregano

1 egg, beaten

½ cup vegetable oil for frying

½ cup panko bread crumbs

½ cup marinara or tomato sauce, heated

1. Trim ends from zucchini; cut in half crosswise. Using spiralizer, spiral zucchini with fine ribbon blade. Pile loosely on cutting board; cut 3 times as if cutting into 6 wedges. Squeeze dry in paper towels if zucchini is very moist. Place in medium bowl. Add flour, salt and oregano; toss until well coated. Add egg; mix until well blended.

2. Heat oil in large skillet over medium-high heat. Place panko in shallow bowl.

3. Working in batches, shape zucchini mixture into 1-inch balls. Place in panko; press panko onto all sides. Place in hot oil. Cook 2 minutes per side or until golden brown.

4. Drain on paper towels. Serve warm with sauce for dipping.

SMALL PLATES

Flatbread with Herbed Ricotta, Peaches and Arugula

Makes 4 servings

- ½ cup ricotta cheese
- 2 tablespoons finely chopped fresh basil
- ½ teaspoon coarse salt
- ⅛ teaspoon black pepper
- 2 whole wheat naan breads
- 1 ripe peach, cut into 12 slices
- ½ cup arugula
- ½ teaspoon lemon juice
- 1 teaspoon extra virgin olive oil
- 2 teaspoons balsamic vinegar
  Flaky sea salt, for garnish

1. Preheat oven to 400°F. Line baking sheet with parchment paper.

2. Combine ricotta cheese, basil, coarse salt and pepper in small bowl. Spread mixture evenly on each piece of naan. Arrange peaches on top. Bake 12 minutes or until bottom of naan is crisp.

3. Combine arugula, lemon juice and oil in medium bowl; toss gently. Top baked flatbreads with arugula. Drizzle with vinegar and sprinkle with sea salt. Cut into pieces to serve.

SMALL PLATES

Simple Bruschetta

Makes 4 servings

1 tablespoon extra virgin olive oil

2 tablespoons thinly sliced red onion

1 clove garlic, minced

1 cup chopped seeded tomato

¼ teaspoon salt

⅛ teaspoon black pepper

Toasted or grilled baguette slices

¼ cup slivered fresh basil

1. Heat oil in medium skillet over medium heat. Add onion; cook and stir 3 minutes. Add garlic; cook and stir 1 minute.

2. Stir in tomato, salt and pepper; let stand 10 minutes. Serve mixture on baguette slices; sprinkle with basil.

Make Ahead: Make tomato mixture ahead of time and let it stand at room temperature for several hours. Do not refrigerate it because the texture of the tomatoes will become mushy.

NF Q EF V DF MA

SMALL PLATES

Cacio e Pepe Cups

Makes 12 cups

8 ounces uncooked spaghetti, broken in half

2 eggs

¼ teaspoon coarsely ground black pepper, plus additional for garnish

¾ cup finely shredded or grated Parmesan cheese, divided

Minced fresh parsley

1. Preheat oven to 350°F. Spray 12 standard (2½-inch) muffin cups with nonstick cooking spray.

2. Cook pasta in large saucepan of boiling salted water until al dente. Drain pasta, reserving about 1 tablespoon cooking water.

3. Meanwhile, whisk eggs and ¼ teaspoon pepper in medium bowl. Stir in ½ cup cheese. Add hot pasta and cooking water; stir until well blended and cheese is melted. Divide spaghetti among prepared muffin cups (tongs work best); pour any remaining egg mixture from bowl into cups. Sprinkle tops with remaining ¼ cup cheese and additional pepper.

4. Bake 15 minutes or until tops are set, no longer shiny and lightly browned. Immediately remove from pan. Sprinkle with parsley; serve warm.

Gluten-Free: Use gluten-free spaghetti or other another long shape in place of the regular spaghetti.

SMALL PLATES

Loaded Nachos

Makes 8 servings

2 teaspoons vegetable oil

1 cup chopped onion

1 tablespoon chili powder

2 teaspoons dried oregano

1 can (15 ounces) pinto beans or black beans, rinsed and drained

48 corn tortilla chips

1¼ cups (5 ounces) shredded Monterey Jack cheese

¾ cup frozen corn, thawed, drained

1 jar (2 ounces) pimientos, drained

3 tablespoons sliced black olives

2 to 3 tablespoons pickled jalapeño pepper slices, drained

1. Heat oil in medium saucepan over medium-high heat. Add onion; cook and stir 8 to 10 minutes or until tender and beginning to brown. Add chili powder and oregano; stir 1 minute.

2. Remove from heat. Add beans and 2 tablespoons water; mash with fork or potato masher until well blended, leaving some beans whole. Return to heat. Cover and cook 6 to 8 minutes or until bubbly and heated through, stirring occasionally. Stir in additional water if beans become dry. Remove from heat.

3. Place chips on large ovenproof pate or baking sheet. Sprinkle cheese evenly over chips. Spoon beans over chips.

4. Combine corn and pimientos in small bowl; spoon over beans. Bake about 8 minutes or until cheese melts. Sprinkle with olives and jalapeños.

Vegan: Use a vegan cheese alternative instead of the Monterey Jack cheese.

PASTA & GRAINS

Spaghetti and Beets Aglio e Olio

Makes 6 servings

1. Using spiralizer, spiral beets with fine spiral blade; cut into desired lengths. Cook spaghetti according to package directions. Drain and return to saucepan, reserving 1/2 cup water; keep warm. Meanwhile, spray large nonstick skillet with nonstick cooking spray; heat over medium-high heat. Add beets; cook and stir 8 to 10 minutes or until tender.

2. Heat 1 tablespoon oil in large skillet over medium heat. Add bread crumbs; cook 4 to 5 minutes or until golden brown, stirring frequently. Transfer to small bowl.

3. Add remaining 1/3 cup oil, garlic, salt and red pepper flakes to same skillet; cook about 3 minutes or until garlic just begins to brown on edges.

4. Add pasta, beets and parsley to skillet; toss to coat with oil mixture. Add some of reserved pasta water to moisten pasta, if desired. Stir in bread crumbs and 1/2 cup cheese. Top with remaining 1/4 cup cheese just before serving.

Gluten-Free: Omit bread crumbs and use gluten-free spaghetti instead of regular.

Vegan: Omit Parmesan cheese.

- 2 **medium beets, peeled**
- 8 **ounces uncooked spaghetti or thin spaghetti**
- 1/3 **cup plus 1 tablespoon olive oil, divided**
- 1 **cup fresh Italian or French bread crumbs***
- 4 **cloves garlic, very thinly sliced**
- 3/4 **teaspoon salt**
- 1/2 **teaspoon red pepper flakes**
- 1/2 **cup chopped fresh Italian parsley**
- 3/4 **cup shredded Parmesan cheese, divided**

*To make fresh bread crumbs, tear 2 ounces bread into pieces; process in food processor until coarse crumbs form.

PASTA & GRAINS

Spinach and Feta Farro Stuffed Peppers

Makes 6 servings

- 1 tablespoon olive oil
- 1 package (5 ounces) baby spinach
- 1/2 cup sliced green onions
- 2 cloves garlic, minced
- 1 tablespoon chopped fresh oregano
- 1 cup pearled farro, cooked according to package directions
- 1 1/2 cups finely chopped seeded fresh tomatoes
- 1/2 teaspoon salt
- 1/8 teaspoon black pepper
- 1 container (4 ounces) crumbled feta cheese, divided
- 3 large bell peppers, halved lengthwise and cored

1. Preheat oven to 350°F.

2. Heat oil in large skillet over medium-high heat. Add spinach, green onions, garlic and oregano; cook 3 minutes, stirring frequently. Stir in farro, tomatoes, salt, black pepper and 1/2 cup cheese.

3. Spoon farro mixture into bell pepper halves (about 3/4 cup each); place in shallow baking pan. Pour 1/4 cup water into bottom of pan; cover with foil.

4. Bake 30 minutes or until bell peppers are crisp-tender and filling is heated through. Sprinkle with remaining cheese.

Make Ahead: Make farro mixture ahead of time and stuff in peppers. Place in pan and cover with plastic wrap. Before baking, add 1/4 cup water to the pan and cover the pan with foil.

PASTA & GRAINS

Soba Miso Bowl

Makes 4 servings

PICKLED CARROTS

- **4 carrots, peeled and shredded or julienned**
- **¼ cup water**
- **¼ cup coarsely chopped ginger (½-inch pieces)**
- **2 tablespoons honey**
- **1 tablespoon salt**
- **½ cup rice vinegar**

MISO DRESSING

- **¼ cup vegetable or peanut oil**
- **2 tablespoons white miso paste**
- **2 tablespoons rice vinegar**
- **2 teaspoons grated fresh ginger**
- **2 teaspoons honey**
- **1 teaspoon dark sesame oil**

BOWLS

- **1 to 2 broccoli crowns, cut into florets**
- **6 ounces uncooked soba noodles**
- **2 cups chopped or shredded red cabbage**
- **Sesame seeds and sprouts (optional)**

1. Place carrots in 1-quart jar or medium bowl. Combine ¼ cup water, chopped ginger, 2 tablespoons honey and salt in small saucepan. Cook and stir over medium heat until salt and honey are dissolved. Pour over carrots. Add ½ cup vinegar. Seal jar; shake to blend. Let stand at room temperature at least 30 minutes or refrigerate until ready to use.

2. For dressing, whisk vegetable oil, miso, 2 tablespoons vinegar, grated ginger, 2 teaspoons honey and sesame oil in small bowl.

3. Bring large saucepan of water to a boil. Add broccoli; cook 3 minutes or until desired doneness. Remove from water with slotted spoon; place in medium bowl. Return water to a boil. Add noodles; reduce heat to medium-low. Cook 3 minutes. Drain in colander; rinse under cold water until cool.

4. For each serving, place noodles, cabbage, broccoli and carrots in bowl. Drizzle with dressing. Garnish with sesame seeds and sprouts.

Vegan: Replace honey with agave nectar or maple syrup.

PASTA & GRAINS

Greek Salad Bowl

Makes 4 servings

1 cup uncooked pearled farro

2½ cups water

1¼ teaspoons dried oregano or Greek seasoning, divided

½ teaspoon salt, divided

¼ cup extra virgin olive oil

2 tablespoons red wine vinegar

1 clove garlic, minced

⅛ teaspoon black pepper (optional)

2 cucumbers, julienned, cubed or thinly sliced

½ red onion, thinly sliced

2 medium tomatoes, diced

1 can (15 ounces) chickpeas, rinsed and drained

4 ounces feta cheese, cubed or crumbled

1. Rinse farro under cold water; place in medium saucepan. Add 2½ cups water, 1 teaspoon oregano and ¼ teaspoon salt. Bring to a boil over high heat. Reduce heat to medium-low; simmer, uncovered, 20 minutes or until farro is tender. Drain any additional water.

2. Whisk oil, vinegar, garlic, remaining ¼ teaspoon salt, remaining ¼ teaspoon oregano and pepper, if desired, in small bowl.

3. Divide farro among 4 bowls; arrange cucumber, onion, tomatoes, chickpeas and feta around farro. Drizzle with dressing.

Make Ahead: This bowl is a great make-ahead option for lunches or future dinners. Add some grilled chicken or lamb for a heartier meal, or mix everything together and serve it as a side dish.

Note: This is a great recipe to use a spiralizer if you have one. Cut the ends off the cucumbers and spiral slice with the thin ribbon blade. Spiral the red onion with the thin ribbon blade and chop into desired pieces.

Vegan: Omit cheese or substitute with cubed extra firm silken tofu.

PASTA & GRAINS

Sesame Noodles

Makes 6 to 8 servings

1 package (16 ounces) uncooked spaghetti

6 tablespoons soy sauce

5 tablespoons dark sesame oil

3 tablespoons sugar

3 tablespoons rice vinegar

2 tablespoons vegetable oil

3 cloves garlic, minced

1 teaspoon grated fresh ginger or ginger paste

1/2 teaspoon sriracha sauce

2 green onions, sliced

1 red bell pepper

1 cucumber

1 carrot

Sesame seeds (optional)

1. Cook spaghetti according to package directions until al dente in large saucepan of boiling salted water. Drain, reserving 1 tablespoon pasta cooking water.

2. Whisk soy sauce, sesame oil, sugar, vinegar, vegetable oil, garlic, ginger, sriracha and reserved pasta water in large bowl. Stir in noodles and green onions. Let stand at least 30 minutes until noodles have cooled to room temperature and most of sauce is absorbed, stirring occasionally.

3. Meanwhile, cut bell pepper into thin strips. Peel cucumber and carrot and shred with julienne peeler into long strands, or cut into thin strips. Stir into noodles. Serve at room temperature or refrigerate until ready to serve. Top with sesame seeds, if desired.

Gluten-Free: Use gluten-free spaghetti instead of regular spaghetti, or use 12 ounces soba noodles cooked according to package directions.

PASTA & GRAINS

Swiss Chard, Barley and Feta Gratin

Makes 8 servings

2/3 cup uncooked quick-cooking barley

12 cups (about 13 ounces) Swiss chard, ends trimmed and leaves and stems cut crosswise in 1/2-inch-wide strips

2 cups water

1 can (about 14 ounces) diced tomatoes, drained

3/4 cup crumbled feta cheese

1/2 teaspoon dried oregano

1/4 teaspoon salt

1/8 teaspoon black pepper

1 tablespoon butter, melted

1/2 teaspoon garlic powder

2/3 cup fresh whole wheat bread crumbs*

1/2 cup vegetable broth

To make fresh bread crumbs, tear 1 1/4 slices bread into pieces; process in food processor until coarse crumbs form.

1. Preheat oven to 375°F. Spray 2-quart baking dish with nonstick cooking spray.

2. Cook barley according to package directions.

3. Place Swiss chard in large saucepan. Add water; cover and bring to a boil. Reduce heat and simmer 13 minutes or until tender. Drain.

4. Combine barley, Swiss chard, tomatoes, cheese, oregano, salt and pepper in prepared baking dish. Spread into even layer.

5. Combine butter and garlic powder in small bowl. Add bread crumbs; mix well. Pour broth over gratin; sprinkle evenly with crumb mixture.

6. Bake 20 minutes or until topping is golden brown. Let stand 5 minutes before serving.

PASTA & GRAINS

Green Bean, Walnut and Blue Cheese Pasta Salad

Makes 4 to 6 servings

2 cups uncooked gemelli pasta

2 cups trimmed halved green beans

3 tablespoons olive oil

2 tablespoons white wine vinegar

1 tablespoon chopped fresh thyme

1 tablespoon Dijon mustard

1 tablespoon fresh lemon juice

1 teaspoon honey

1/4 teaspoon salt

1/4 teaspoon black pepper

1/2 cup chopped walnuts, toasted*

1/2 cup crumbled blue cheese

To toast walnuts, spread in single layer in heavy skillet. Cook over medium heat 1 to 2 minutes until nuts are lightly browned, stirring frequently. Remove from skillet immediately. Cool before using.

1. Cook pasta according to package directions in large saucepan of boiling salted water. Add green beans during the last 4 minutes of cooking. Drain. Transfer to large bowl.

2. Meanwhile, whisk oil, vinegar, thyme, mustard, lemon juice, honey, salt and pepper in medium bowl until smooth and well blended.

3. Pour dressing over pasta and green beans; toss to coat evenly. Stir in walnuts and cheese. Serve warm or cover and refrigerate until ready to serve.**

**If serving cold, stir walnuts into salad just before serving.

Gluten-Free: Use any gluten-free pasta shape instead of the regular gemelli.

Vegan: Omit the cheese and substitute agave nectar for the honey.

PASTA & GRAINS

Vegetable Rice Noodles

Makes 4 servings

8 ounces thin rice noodles (rice vermicelli)

½ cup soy sauce

⅓ cup sugar

¼ cup lime juice

2 fresh red Thai chiles or 1 large jalapeño pepper, finely chopped

¼ cup vegetable oil

8 ounces firm tofu, drained and cut into triangles

1 jicama (8 ounces), peeled and chopped or 1 can (8 ounces) sliced water chestnuts, drained

2 medium sweet potatoes (1 pound), peeled and cut into ¼-inch-thick slices

2 large leeks, cut into ¼-inch-thick slices

¼ cup chopped dry-roasted peanuts

2 tablespoons chopped fresh mint

2 tablespoons chopped fresh cilantro

1. Place rice noodles in medium bowl. Cover with hot water; let stand 15 minutes or until soft. Drain well; cut into 3-inch lengths.

2. Combine soy sauce, sugar, lime juice and chiles in small bowl until well blended; set aside.

3. Meanwhile, heat oil in large skillet over medium-high heat. Add tofu; cook and stir 4 minutes per side or until golden brown. Remove with slotted spatula to paper towel-lined wire rack.

4. Add jicama to skillet; cook and stir 5 minutes or until lightly browned. Remove to baking sheet. Cook sweet potatoes in batches until tender and browned, turning once. Remove to wire rack. Add leeks; cook and stir 1 minute; remove to wire rack.

5. Stir soy sauce mixture; add to skillet. Heat until sugar dissolves. Add noodles; toss to coat. Gently stir in tofu, vegetables, peanuts, mint and cilantro.

Make Ahead: Leftovers make a great lunch. Have them cold or warm them briefly in the microwave.

    MA

PASTA & GRAINS

Penne Italiano

Makes 4 servings

- 1 tablespoon olive oil
- 1 red bell pepper, cut into ½-inch pieces
- 1 green bell pepper, cut into ½-inch pieces
- 1 medium sweet onion, halved and thinly sliced
- 3 cloves garlic, minced
- 2 tablespoons tomato paste
- 2 teaspoons salt
- 1 teaspoon sugar
- 1 teaspoon Italian seasoning
- ¼ teaspoon black pepper
- 1 can (28 ounces) Italian plum tomatoes, chopped, juice reserved
- 8 ounces uncooked penne pasta

  Grated Parmesan cheese

  Chopped fresh basil

1. Heat oil in large skillet over medium-high heat. Add bell peppers, onion and garlic; cook and stir 8 minutes or until vegetables are crisp-tender.

2. Add tomato paste, salt, sugar, Italian seasoning and black pepper; cook 1 minute. Stir in tomatoes with juice. Reduce heat to medium-low; cook 15 minutes or until vegetables are tender and sauce is thickened.

3. Meanwhile, cook pasta in large saucepan of boiling salted water according to package directions until al dente. Drain pasta; return to saucepan. Add sauce; stir gently to coat. Divide among 4 serving bowls; top with cheese and basil.

Vegan: Omit cheese and top with nutritional yeast, if desired.

Gluten-Free: Use any gluten-free pasta shape instead of the regular penne.

PASTA & GRAINS

Farro, Grape and Roasted Carrot Bowl

Makes 4 to 6 servings

1 pound carrots, peeled, trimmed and halved lengthwise

3 tablespoons extra virgin olive oil, divided

1 teaspoon salt, divided

1/2 teaspoon ground cumin

1/4 teaspoon ground coriander

1/8 teaspoon ground nutmeg

1 package (about 2 1/4 ounces) slivered almonds

2 cups water

1 cup uncooked pearled farro, rinsed under cold water

2 tablespoons balsamic vinegar

Salt and black pepper

1 cup halved red grapes

1/4 cup minced red onion

4 cups mixed spring greens

1. Preheat oven to 375°F. Place carrots on sheet pan. Drizzle with 1 tablespoon oil. Combine 1/2 teaspoon salt, cumin, coriander and nutmeg in small bowl; sprinkle over carrots. Toss to coat carrots with oil and spices. Arrange cut sides down in single layer.

2. Roast 30 minutes or until carrots are browned and tender, turning once. Place almonds on small baking sheet; bake about 5 minutes or until almonds are toasted, stirring frequently.

3. Meanwhile, bring 2 cups water and remaining 1/2 teaspoon salt to a boil in medium saucepan. Stir in farro; reduce heat to medium-low. Cover and simmer 20 to 25 minutes or until tender. Drain and place farro in large bowl.

4. Whisk remaining 2 tablespoons oil into vinegar in small bowl; pour over farro. Stir in grapes and onion; season to taste with additional salt and pepper. Cut carrots into 1-inch pieces; add to farro mixture. Place greens in serving bowls; top with farro salad and sprinkle with almonds.

   (MA)

SANDWICHES & TOASTS

Tuscan Portobello Melt

Makes 2 servings

1. Preheat broiler. Combine mushroom, onion and tomatoes in small baking pan. Drizzle with oil and vinegar; sprinkle with salt, thyme and pepper. Toss to coat. Spread vegetables in single layer in pan.

2. Broil 6 minutes or until vegetables are softened and browned, stirring once.

3. Heat medium skillet over medium heat. Spread 1 tablespoon butter over one side of each bread slice. Place buttered side down in skillet; cook 2 minutes or until bread is toasted. Transfer bread to cutting board, toasted sides up.

4. Place provolone cheese on 2 bread slices; spread mustard over cheese. Top with vegetables, Monterey Jack cheese and remaining bread slices, toasted sides down. Spread remaining 1 tablespoon butter on outside of sandwiches. Cook in same skillet over medium heat 5 minutes or until bread is toasted and cheese is melted, turning once.

- 1 **portobello mushroom cap, thinly sliced**
- 1/2 **small red onion, thinly sliced**
- 1/2 **cup grape tomatoes**
- 1 **tablespoon olive oil**
- 1 **teaspoon balsamic vinegar**
- 1/8 **teaspoon salt**
- 1/8 **teaspoon dried thyme**
- 1/8 **teaspoon black pepper**
- 2 **tablespoons butter, softened, divided**
- 4 **slices sourdough bread**
- 2 **slices provolone cheese**
- 2 **teaspoons Dijon mustard**
- 2 **slices Monterey Jack cheese**

SANDWICHES & TOASTS

Hearty Veggie Sandwich

Makes 4 servings

1 **pound cremini mushrooms, stemmed and thinly sliced ($1/8$-inch slices)**

2 **tablespoons olive oil, divided**

$3/4$ **teaspoon salt, divided**

$1/4$ **teaspoon black pepper**

1 **medium zucchini, diced ($1/4$-inch pieces, about 2 cups)**

3 **tablespoons butter, softened**

8 **slices artisan whole grain bread**

$1/4$ **cup prepared pesto**

$1/4$ **cup mayonnaise**

2 **cups packed baby spinach**

4 **slices (about 1 ounce each) mozzarella cheese**

1. Preheat oven to 350°F. Combine mushrooms, 1 tablespoon oil, $1/2$ teaspoon salt and pepper in medium bowl; toss to coat. Spread on large rimmed baking sheet. Roast 20 minutes or until mushrooms are dark brown and dry, stirring after 10 minutes. Cool on baking sheet.

2. Meanwhile, heat remaining 1 tablespoon oil in large skillet over medium heat. Add zucchini and remaining $1/4$ teaspoon salt; cook and stir 5 minutes or until zucchini is tender and lightly browned. Transfer to bowl; wipe out skillet with paper towels.

3. Spread butter over one side of each bread slice; turn over. Spread pesto over 4 slices; spread mayonnaise over remaining 4 slices. Top pesto-covered slices evenly with mushrooms, then spinach, zucchini and cheese. Top with remaining bread slices, mayonnaise side down.

4. Heat same skillet over medium heat. Add sandwiches; cover and cook 2 minutes per side or until bread is toasted, spinach is slightly wilted and cheese is beginning to melt. Cut sandwiches in half; serve immediately.

SANDWICHES & TOASTS

Curried Quinoa Burgers

Makes 6 servings

½ cup uncooked quinoa, rinsed well in fine-mesh strainer

½ cup red lentils, rinsed well in fine-mesh strainer

1½ cups water

1½ teaspoons salt, divided

3 tablespoons olive oil, divided

1 medium onion, diced

½ cup frozen peas

3 cloves garlic, minced

2 teaspoons curry powder

1 egg

6 gluten-free or regular hamburger buns

Lettuce, sliced tomatoes, thinly sliced red onion, mango chutney (optional)

1. Combine quinoa, lentils, water and ½ teaspoon salt in large saucepan. Bring to a boil over medium-high heat. Reduce heat to low; cover and simmer 15 minutes or until quinoa and lentils are tender. Drain any excess liquid. Place in large bowl.

2. Heat 1 tablespoon oil in large nonstick skillet over medium-high heat. Add onion and remaining 1 teaspoon salt; cook and stir 5 minutes or until onion is softened. Reduce heat to medium. Add peas; cook and stir 4 minutes. Add garlic and curry powder; cook and stir 30 seconds. Add to quinoa mixture with egg; mix well. Cool 15 minutes.

3. Scoop mixture by ½ cupfuls; shape into ½-inch-thick patties. If making ahead, place patties on baking sheet or large plate sprayed with nonstick cooking spray and refrigerate until ready to cook.

4. Heat 1 tablespoon oil in skillet over medium-high heat. Reduce heat to medium; gently place patties in skillet. Cook 4 to 5 minutes or until well browned on bottom. Add remaining 1 tablespoon oil to skillet, flip patties and continue cooking 4 to 5 minutes or until browned on other side. Serve on buns with desired toppings.

SANDWICHES & TOASTS

Spinach Veggie Wrap

Makes 4 servings

PICO DE GALLO

- 1 **cup finely chopped tomatoes (about 2 small)**
- 1/2 **teaspoon salt**
- 1/4 **cup chopped white onion**
- 2 **tablespoons minced jalapeño pepper**
- 2 **tablespoons chopped fresh cilantro**
- 1 **teaspoon lime juice**

GUACAMOLE

- 2 **large ripe avocados, halved and pitted**
- 1/4 **cup finely chopped red onion**
- 2 **tablespoons chopped fresh cilantro**
- 2 **teaspoons lime juice**
- 1/2 **teaspoon salt**

WRAPS

- 4 **whole wheat burrito-size tortillas (about 10 inches)**
- 2 **cups fresh baby spinach leaves**
- 1 **cup sliced mushrooms**
- 1 **cup shredded Asiago cheese**
- **Salsa**

1. For pico de gallo, combine tomatoes and 1/2 teaspoon salt in fine-mesh strainer; set in bowl or sink to drain 15 minutes. Combine drained tomatoes, white onion, jalapeño, 2 tablespoons cilantro and 1 teaspoon lime juice in medium bowl; mix well.

2. For guacamole, scoop avocado into another medium bowl. Add red onion, 2 tablespoons cilantro, 2 teaspoons lime juice and 1/2 teaspoon salt; mash with fork to desired consistency.

3. For wraps, spread 1/4 cup guacamole on each tortilla. Layer each with 1/2 cup spinach, 1/4 cup mushrooms, 1/4 cup cheese and 1/4 cup pico de gallo. Roll up; serve with salsa.

Vegan: Omit cheese or use a vegan cheese alternative.

Make Ahead: Wraps make great packed lunches. Prepare the pico de gallo and guacamole ahead of time and store them in the refrigerator. Assemble the wraps as you need them and wrap them in plastic wrap to go.

SANDWICHES & TOASTS

Mediterranean Vegetable Sandwich

Makes 4 sandwiches

- ½ cup plain hummus
- ½ jalapeño pepper, seeded and minced
- ¼ cup minced fresh cilantro
- 8 slices whole wheat bread
- 4 leaves lettuce (leaf or Bibb lettuce)
- 2 tomatoes, thinly sliced
- ½ cucumber, thinly sliced
- ½ red onion, thinly sliced
- ½ cup thinly sliced peppadew peppers or sweet Italian peppers
- 4 tablespoons crumbled feta cheese

1. Combine hummus, jalapeño and cilantro in small bowl; mix well.

2. Spread about 1 tablespoon hummus mixture on one side of each bread slice. Layer half of bread slices with lettuce, tomatoes, cucumber, onion, peppadew peppers and feta; top with remaining bread slices. Cut sandwiches in half.

Vegan: Omit feta cheese.

SANDWICHES & TOASTS

Black Bean Burgers with Spicy Mayo

Makes 4 servings

5 whole wheat hamburger buns (1½ to 2 ounces each), split, divided

1 can (15 ounces) black beans, rinsed and well drained

½ cup (2 ounces) Cheddar cheese or Mexican blend cheese

2 egg whites

2 green onions, sliced

1 teaspoon chili powder

1 teaspoon dried oregano

½ teaspoon garlic salt

1 tablespoon canola oil

2 tablespoons mayonnaise

¾ teaspoon chipotle hot pepper sauce

Lettuce and tomato slices

1. Tear 1 hamburger bun into pieces; place in bowl of food processor. Process until coarse crumbs form. Transfer to medium bowl.

2. Add beans, cheese, egg whites, green onions, chili powder, oregano and garlic salt to food processor. Process to a thick paste, scraping down sides of bowl once. Add mixture to bread crumbs in bowl; mix well.

3. Heat oil in large nonstick skillet over medium heat. Scoop mixture into 4 mounds in skillet by by ½ cupfuls; press down to form 4-inch patties. Cook 4 minutes per side or until browned. Lightly toast remaining hamburger buns, if desired.

4. Combine mayonnaise and hot pepper sauce in small bowl. Serve patties in buns with mayonnaise mixture, lettuce and tomato.

SANDWICHES & TOASTS

Avocado Toast

Makes 2 servings

- ½ cup thawed frozen peas
- 2 teaspoons lemon juice
- 1 teaspoon minced fresh tarragon
- ¼ teaspoon plus ⅛ teaspoon salt, divided
- ⅛ teaspoon black pepper
- 1 teaspoon olive oil
- 1 tablespoon pepitas (raw pumpkin seeds)
- 4 slices hearty whole grain bread, toasted
- 1 avocado

1. Combine peas, lemon juice, tarragon, ¼ teaspoon salt and pepper in small food processor; pulse until blended but still chunky. Or combine all ingredients in small bowl and mash with fork to desired consistency.

2. Heat oil in small saucepan over medium heat. Add pepitas; cook and stir 1 to 2 minutes or until toasted. Transfer to small bowl; stir in remaining ⅛ teaspoon salt.

3. Spread about 1 tablespoon pea mixture over each slice of bread. If making one serving, place the remaining pea mixture in a jar or container and store in the refrigerator for a day or two.

4. Cut avocado in half lengthwise around pit. If making one serving, wrap the half with the pit in plastic wrap and store in the refrigerator for a day. Cut the avocado into slices in the shell; use a spoon to scoop the slices out of the shell. Arrange avocado slices on the toast; top with toasted pepitas.

Southwestern Flatbread with Black Beans and Corn

Makes 4 servings

2 oval flatbreads (11×7 inches)

¼ cup prepared green chile enchilada sauce

2 cups (8 ounces) shredded Monterey Jack cheese

1 can (15 ounces) black beans, rinsed and drained

1 cup frozen corn, thawed

½ cup finely chopped red onion

1 teaspoon olive oil

½ teaspoon kosher salt

1 avocado, diced

2 tablespoons fresh chopped cilantro

Lime wedges (optional)

1. Preheat oven to 425°F. Place wire rack on large baking sheet; place flatbreads on rack.

2. Spread enchilada sauce over flatbreads; sprinkle with cheese. Combine beans, corn, onion, oil and salt in medium bowl. Layer mixture on top of cheese. Bake 12 minutes or until flatbreads are golden and crisp and cheese is melted.

3. Arrange avocado on flatbreads; sprinkle with cilantro. Cut into pieces to serve. Serve with lime wedges, if desired.

SANDWICHES & TOASTS

Chickpea, Roasted Pepper and Olive Toasts

Makes 24 toasts

2 cloves garlic, peeled

1 can (15 ounces) chickpeas, rinsed and drained

1 cup chopped drained roasted red peppers

1/4 cup olive oil

Salt and black pepper

1/2 cup drained pitted black olives

1/2 cup drained pimiento-stuffed green olives

24 (1/2-inch) toasted French bread slices

1. Turn on food processor; drop garlic through feed tube. Add chickpeas and roasted peppers; process until paste forms. With motor running, add oil in thin steady stream; process until smooth. Transfer chickpea mixture to medium bowl; season with salt and black pepper. Cover and let stand 30 minutes.

2. Place black and green olives in clean food processor. Pulse until olives are coarsely chopped.

3. Spread 2 tablespoons chickpea mixture on each bread slice. Spoon 1 tablespoon olive mixture in center of chickpea mixture. Serve at room temperature.

Note: Leftover chickpea mixture makes a great dip for fresh vegetables.

Make-Ahead: Chickpea and olive mixtures can both be prepared up to 2 days in advance. Store separately in airtight containers in the refrigerator.

VEGETABLES & BEANS

Zoodles in Tomato Sauce

Makes 4 servings

1. Heat 2 teaspoons oil in medium saucepan over medium heat. Add garlic; cook 1 minute or until fragrant but not browned. Stir in tomato paste; cook 30 seconds, stirring constantly. Add tomatoes with juice, oregano and salt; break up tomatoes with wooden spoon. Bring to a simmer. Reduce heat; cook 30 minutes or until thickened.

2. Meanwhile, spiral zucchini with fine spiral blade. Heat remaining 1 teaspoon oil in large skillet over medium-high heat. Add zucchini; cook 4 to 5 minutes or until tender, stirring frequently. Transfer to serving plates; top with tomato sauce and Parmesan cheese, if desired.

Note: If you don't have a spiralizer, buy packaged zucchini noodles from the produce section of large supermarkets. Or cut the zucchini into ribbons with a mandoline, a julienne peeler or sharp knife.

Vegan: Omit Parmesan cheese.

- 3 **teaspoons olive oil, divided**
- 2 **cloves garlic**
- 1 **tablespoon tomato paste**
- 1 **can (28 ounces) whole tomatoes, undrained**
- 1 **teaspoon dried oregano**
- ½ **teaspoon salt**
- 2 **large zucchini (about 16 ounces each), ends trimmed, cut into 3-inch pieces**
- ¼ **cup shredded Parmesan cheese**

Jalapeño Beans

Makes 4 to 6 servings

- 1 tablespoon vegetable oil
- 1 small onion, finely chopped
- 1 teaspoon ground cumin
- 1 teaspoon garlic powder
- 1/2 teaspoon smoked paprika
- 1/4 teaspoon ground red pepper
- 3 tablespoons chopped pickled jalapeño peppers
- 2 cans (15 ounces each) chili beans (made with pinto beans)
- 1/3 cup dark lager beer
- 1 tablespoon white vinegar
- 1 teaspoon sugar
- 1/2 teaspoon hot pepper sauce

  Salt and black pepper

1. Heat oil in medium saucepan over medium-high heat. Add onion; cook and stir 2 minutes or until translucent. Add cumin, garlic powder, paprika and red pepper; cook and stir 1 minute. Add pickled jalapeños; cook and stir 30 seconds.

2. Stir in beans, beer, vinegar, sugar and hot pepper sauce; bring to a boil. Reduce heat to medium-low; cook 15 minutes, stirring occasionally. Season with salt and black pepper. Beans will thicken upon standing.

Pesto Rice and Beans

Makes 8 servings

2 cans (handwritten)

1 can (15 ounces) Great Northern beans, ~~rinsed and drained~~

1 can (about 14 ounces) *MORE* (handwritten) vegetable broth

³/₄ cup uncooked long-grain white rice

1¹/₂ cups frozen cut green beans, thawed and drained *bag* (handwritten)

¹/₂ cup prepared pesto

Grated Parmesan cheese (optional)

a little mushy (handwritten)

SLOW COOKER DIRECTIONS

1. Combine Great Northern beans, broth and rice in slow cooker. Cover; cook on LOW 2 hours.

2. Stir in green beans; cover and cook on LOW 1 hour or until rice and beans are tender.

3. Turn off slow cooker and remove insert to heatproof surface. Stir in pesto and Parmesan cheese, if desired. Let stand, covered, 5 minutes or until cheese is melted. Serve immediately.

VEGETABLES & BEANS

Roasted Balsamic Asparagus

Makes 6 servings

- 1 **pound fresh asparagus**
- 1 **tablespoon olive oil**
- 1/2 **teaspoon salt**
- 1/4 **teaspoon black pepper**
- 1 **tablespoon balsamic glaze***
- 1/4 **cup finely shredded or grated Parmesan cheese**

Balsamic glaze can be found in the condiment section of the supermarket or can be prepared by simmering 2 tablespoons balsamic vinegar in small saucepan until reduced by about half.

1. Preheat oven to 375°F.

2. Arrange asparagus in single layer in shallow 11×7-inch baking dish. Drizzle asparagus with oil; gently roll to coat evenly. Sprinkle with salt and pepper.

3. Bake 14 to 16 minutes or until crisp-tender. Drizzle balsamic glaze over asparagus; roll again with tongs to coat. Top with cheese.

Vegan: Omit Parmesan cheese.

NF Q GF EF

Red Beans and Rice with Pickled Carrots and Cucumbers

Makes 6 servings

Pickled Carrots and Cucumbers (page 113)

1 pound dried red kidney beans

1 tablespoon plus 1 teaspoon salt, divided

2 tablespoons olive oil

2 onions, chopped

3 stalks celery, chopped

1 green bell pepper, chopped

4 cloves garlic, minced

4 cups vegetable broth

1 teaspoon liquid smoke

1 bay leaf

2 teaspoons Italian seasoning

$1/2$ teaspoon black pepper

$1/4$ teaspoon ground red pepper

$1/2$ cup water

Hot cooked brown rice

Sliced avocado

Hot pepper sauce

1. Prepare pickled carrots and cucumbers. Place beans in large bowl. Cover with water and stir in 1 tablespoon salt. Soak 8 hours or overnight. Drain.

2. Heat oil in large saucepan over medium-high heat. Add onions; cook and stir 5 minutes. Season with remaining 1 teaspoon salt. Add celery, bell pepper and garlic; cook and stir 5 minutes or until vegetables are tender.

3. Add beans, broth, liquid smoke, bay leaf, Italian seasoning, black pepper and red pepper; bring to a boil. Reduce heat; simmer, partially covered, 45 minutes. Remove 2 cups bean mixture to medium bowl; let stand 15 minutes to cool slightly. Place in blender or food processor and add $1/2$ cup water; blend until smooth. Stir into beans; continue to cook until beans are tender. Taste and season with additional salt, if desired. Remove and discard bay leaf. Serve with pickled vegetables, rice, avocado and hot pepper sauce.

NF GF EF V DF MA

Pickled Carrots
and Cucumbers

2 **carrots**

1 **cucumber**

¼ **cup water**

2 **tablespoons sugar**

1 **tablespoon salt**

1 **teaspoon peppercorns**

2 **cloves garlic, smashed**

¼ **teaspoon dried dill**

2 **bay leaves**

1½ **cups white vinegar**

1. Thinly slice carrots into coins. Very thinly slice cucumber (¹⁄₁₆-inch slices) with a mandoline if you have one or a sharp knife. Place carrots and cucumbers in 1-quart jar.

2. Combine water, sugar, salt, peppercorns, garlic, dill and bay leaves in small saucepan. Cook over medium heat until salt and sugar are dissolved. Pour over vegetables in jar. Add enough vinegar to cover. Seal jar and refrigerate at least 2 hours. Can be made a few days in advance.

VEGETABLES & BEANS

Fried Green Tomato Parmesan

Makes 4 servings

2 cans (15 ounces each) tomato sauce

4 green tomatoes, thickly sliced into 3 slices each

1/2 teaspoon salt, divided

Black pepper

1/2 cup all-purpose flour

1 teaspoon Italian seasoning

2 eggs

2 tablespoons water

1 1/2 cups panko bread crumbs

4 tablespoons olive oil, divided

1/2 cup shredded Parmesan cheese

Shredded fresh basil

Hot cooked spaghetti (optional)

1. Preheat oven to 350°F. Spread 1 cup tomato sauce in 9-inch square baking dish. Sprinkle one side of tomatoes with 1/4 teaspoon salt; season lightly with pepper.

2. Combine flour, Italian seasoning and remaining 1/4 teaspoon salt in shallow bowl. Whisk eggs and water in another shallow bowl. Place panko in third shallow bowl. Coat tomatoes with flour mixture. Dip in egg mixture, letting excess drip back into bowl. Dredge in panko, pressing onto all sides.

3. Heat 2 tablespoons oil in large skillet over medium-high heat. Add half of tomatoes; cook 3 minutes per side or until panko is golden brown. Arrange tomatoes in single layer in sauce in baking dish. Sprinkle 1 teaspoon cheese on each tomato; spread some sauce over tomatoes. Heat remaining 2 tablespoons oil in same skillet; cook remaining tomatoes 3 minutes per side until coating is golden brown. Stagger tomatoes in second layer over tomatoes in baking dish. Top each tomato with 1 teaspoon cheese and spread 1 cup sauce over top. Sprinkle with remaining cheese.

4. Bake 20 minutes or until cheese is melted and sauce is heated through. Heat remaining tomato sauce. Serve tomatoes with basil, sauce and spaghetti, if desired.

NF

VEGETABLES & BEANS

Smashed Potatoes

Makes 4 servings

- 4 medium russet potatoes (about 1½ pounds), peeled and cut into ¼-inch cubes
- ⅓ cup milk
- 2 tablespoons sour cream
- 1 tablespoon minced onion
- ½ teaspoon salt
- ¼ teaspoon black pepper
- ⅛ teaspoon garlic powder (optional)
- Chopped fresh chives (optional)

1. Bring large saucepan of lightly salted water to a boil. Add potatoes; cook 15 to 20 minutes or until fork-tender. Drain and return to saucepan.

2. Slightly mash potatoes. Stir in milk, sour cream, minced onion, salt, pepper and garlic powder, if desired. Mash until desired texture is reached, leaving potatoes chunky. Cook 5 minutes over low heat until heated through, stirring occasionally. Top with chives, if desired.

VEGETABLES & BEANS

Garlic-Cilantro Green Beans

Makes 4 to 6 servings

1½ **pounds green beans, ends trimmed**

3 **tablespoons olive oil**

1 **red bell pepper, cut into thin strips**

½ **sweet onion, halved and thinly sliced**

2 **teaspoons minced garlic**

1 **teaspoon salt**

2 **tablespoons chopped fresh cilantro**

Black pepper

1. Bring large saucepan of salted water to a boil over medium-high heat. Add beans; cook 6 minutes or until tender. Drain and return to saucepan.

2. Meanwhile, heat oil in large skillet over medium-high heat. Add bell pepper and onion; cook and stir 3 minutes or until vegetables are tender but not browned. Add garlic; cook and stir 30 seconds. Add beans and salt; cook and stir 2 minutes or until heated through and beans are coated with oil. Stir in cilantro; season with black pepper. Serve immediately.

VEGETABLES & BEANS

Mexican-Style Corn on the Cob

Makes 4 servings

- ¼ cup mayonnaise
- 1 teaspoon chili powder
- 1 teaspoon grated lime peel
- 4 ears corn, shucked
- ¼ cup grated cotija or Parmesan cheese

1. Prepare grill for direct cooking. Combine mayonnaise, chili powder and lime peel in small bowl.

2. Grill corn over medium-high heat 4 to 6 minutes or until lightly charred, turning occasionally. Immediately spread mayonnaise mixture over corn. Sprinkle with cheese.

Note: Corn can be broiled or cooked in a dry cast iron skillet instead of grilling. Or remove the kernels from the cobs and cook 2 minutes in lightly salted boiling water. Drain well, place in a medium bowl and stir in the remaining ingredients.

VEGETABLES & BEANS

Channa Chat (Indian-Spiced Snack Mix)

Makes 6 to 8 servings

- 2 teaspoons canola oil
- 1 medium onion, finely chopped, divided
- 2 cloves garlic, minced
- 2 cans (15 ounces each) chickpeas, rinsed and drained
- ¼ cup vegetable broth or water
- 2 teaspoons tomato paste
- ¼ teaspoon ground cinnamon
- ¼ teaspoon ground cumin
- ¼ teaspoon black pepper
- 1 bay leaf
- ½ cup balsamic vinegar
- 1 tablespoon packed brown sugar
- 1 plum tomato, chopped
- ½ jalapeño pepper, minced *or* ¼ teaspoon ground red pepper (optional)
- ½ cup crisp rice cereal
- 3 tablespoons chopped fresh cilantro (optional)

SLOW COOKER DIRECTIONS

1. Heat oil in small skillet over medium heat. Add half of onion and garlic; cook and stir 2 minutes or until softened. Transfer to slow cooker. Stir in chickpeas, broth, tomato paste, cinnamon, cumin, black pepper and bay leaf.

2. Cover; cook on LOW 6 hours or on HIGH 3 hours. Remove and discard bay leaf.

3. Transfer chickpeas to large shallow bowl with slotted spoon; let cool 15 minutes. Meanwhile, combine balsamic vinegar and brown sugar in small saucepan. Cook over medium-low heat until mixture becomes syrupy.

4. Toss chickpeas with tomato, remaining onion and jalapeño, if desired. Fold in rice cereal and drizzle with balsamic syrup. Garnish with cilantro.

Layered Mexican-Style Casserole

Makes 6 servings

2 cans (15 ounces each) hominy, drained*

1 can (15 ounces) black beans, rinsed and drained

1 can (about 14 ounces) diced tomatoes with garlic, basil and oregano

1 cup thick and chunky salsa

1 can (6 ounces) tomato paste

½ teaspoon ground cumin

¼ teaspoon salt

3 (9-inch) flour tortillas

2 cups (8 ounces) shredded Monterey Jack cheese

¼ cup sliced black olives

Hominy is corn that has been treated to remove the germ and hull. It can be found with the canned vegetables or beans in most supermarkets.

SLOW COOKER DIRECTIONS

1. Prepare foil handles (see below). Spray inside of slow cooker with nonstick cooking spray.

2. Combine hominy, beans, tomatoes, salsa, tomato paste, cumin and salt in large bowl.

3. Press 1 tortilla in bottom of slow cooker. (Edges of tortilla may turn up slightly.) Top with one third of hominy mixture and one third of cheese. Repeat layers. Press remaining tortilla on top. Top with remaining hominy mixture. Set aside remaining cheese.

4. Cover; cook on LOW 6 to 8 hours. Sprinkle with remaining cheese and olives. Cover; let stand 5 minutes. Pull out tortilla stack with foil handles. Cut into wedges.

Foil Handles: Tear off three (18×2-inch) strips of heavy-duty foil or use regular foil folded to double thickness. Crisscross foil strips in spoke design and place into slow cooker to make removing the tortilla stack easier.

Gluten-Free: Use corn tortillas instead of flour tortillas.

INDEX

METRIC CONVERSION CHART

VOLUME MEASUREMENTS (dry)

1/8 teaspoon = 0.5 mL
1/4 teaspoon = 1 mL
1/2 teaspoon = 2 mL
3/4 teaspoon = 4 mL
1 teaspoon = 5 mL
1 tablespoon = 15 mL
2 tablespoons = 30 mL
1/4 cup = 60 mL
1/3 cup = 75 mL
1/2 cup = 125 mL
2/3 cup = 150 mL
3/4 cup = 175 mL
1 cup = 250 mL
2 cups = 1 pint = 500 mL
3 cups = 750 mL
4 cups = 1 quart = 1 L

VOLUME MEASUREMENTS (fluid)

1 fluid ounce (2 tablespoons) = 30 mL
4 fluid ounces (1/2 cup) = 125 mL
8 fluid ounces (1 cup) = 250 mL
12 fluid ounces (1 1/2 cups) = 375 mL
16 fluid ounces (2 cups) = 500 mL

WEIGHTS (mass)

1/2 ounce = 15 g
1 ounce = 30 g
3 ounces = 90 g
4 ounces = 120 g
8 ounces = 225 g
10 ounces = 285 g
12 ounces = 360 g
16 ounces = 1 pound = 450 g

DIMENSIONS

1/16 inch = 2 mm
1/8 inch = 3 mm
1/4 inch = 6 mm
1/2 inch = 1.5 cm
3/4 inch = 2 cm
1 inch = 2.5 cm

OVEN TEMPERATURES

250°F = 120°C
275°F = 140°C
300°F = 150°C
325°F = 160°C
350°F = 180°C
375°F = 190°C
400°F = 200°C
425°F = 220°C
450°F = 230°C

BAKING PAN SIZES

Utensil	Size in Inches/Quarts	Metric Volume	Size in Centimeters
Baking or Cake Pan (square or rectangular)	8×8×2	2 L	20×20×5
	9×9×2	2.5 L	23×23×5
	12×8×2	3 L	30×20×5
	13×9×2	3.5 L	33×23×5
Loaf Pan	8×4×3	1.5 L	20×10×7
	9×5×3	2 L	23×13×7
Round Layer Cake Pan	8×1½	1.2 L	20×4
	9×1½	1.5 L	23×4
Pie Plate	8×1¼	750 mL	20×3
	9×1¼	1 L	23×3
Baking Dish or Casserole	1 quart	1 L	—
	1½ quart	1.5 L	—
	2 quart	2 L	—